# You Are Successful

Wes Lee

Published by Wes Lee, 2020.

YOU ARE SUCCESSFUL

**First edition. September 3, 2020.**

Written by Wes Lee.

# Also by Wes Lee

Impactful Leadership

You Have A Purpose

You Are Rich

You Are Free

Professional Persuasion

The Brave Bunch (Children's Book)

Watch for more at amazon.com/author/wes_lee

I dedicate this book to you. Your commitment to personal success inspires me.

.

# Contents

# Introduction

Have you ever wondered why moving forward can be so tricky? The truth's that hugely successful people are very disciplined. And, there are successful habits you can adopt to achieve the same success. We're creatures of habit, everything we think, say and do, results from deeply rooted patterns in our minds; through years of repetitive behavior. Those same habits move us forward or impede our progress in life. The state and quality of our life right now is a direct reflection of our practices. Our patterns are an essential part of life. They are an integral part of the behaviors that shape our lives. They're so important that one study determined that about 45 percent of everything we do is habitual. Separating ourselves from our bad habits and replacing them with good habits doesn't need to be hard. However, it requires willpower, commitment, and a desire to overcome our natural tendencies to think, listen, speak, and act how we do.

Many people wonder how to get the success they want. They wonder what they're missing. What these people don't realize is that they already have all the resources to get what they want. Successful people are where they are today because of their habits; habits determine 95 percent of a person's behavior. Everything you are today and everything you'll achieve comes from the quality of your habits. Model successful practices, adopt a positive character, and you can live a prosperous life with everything you want.

# CHAPTER ONE

## What is a habit?

Habits are the small decisions and actions you take every day. Your habits account for about 40 percent of your behavior, and your life's the sum of them. Everyone has habits, good or bad! You began developing habits from a young age, such as sucking a thumb, napping every afternoon, or leaving the lights on. These behaviors are part of our routines.

Do you see the power of a habit? Take a moment and list some of your most essential practices. What patterns would you like to keep? Which ones do you want to remove? We know that not all habits are good for us. Many of us recognize the need to get rid of bad habits or cultivate new habits that empower us. And that's why we seek guidance through self-help books, the internet, advice from friends, family, and consultants. A "habit" in psychology, is any regularly repeated behavior that requires little or no thought; it's learned rather than innate. A pattern can be part of any activity, from eating and sleeping to thinking and reacting. Patterns will develop through reinforcement and repetition. *Reinforcing* encourages the *repetition* of a behavior or response. Every time the stimulus is triggered, the action occurs. The practice becomes more automatic with each repetition. However, some habits can be formed based on a single experience, usually when emotions are involved.

# How do habits influence our success?

Your habits show your unique identity to the world. However, sometimes people forget that their habits also affect their success. It's essential to know how your patterns change how you succeed. Your practices reflect who you are and form your unique identity. For example, some people get up early, while others sleep-in. Your sleep patterns a habit that starts your day. And we get so used to the daily routines that we don't realize they're influencing our lives. If someone wants to be successful, they need to think about everything they do or don't do. Each of their practices shows their commitment. Being successful depends mostly on the habits you engage in repeatedly, which ultimately shapes your life. Your habits will make or break your existence, as they directly influence your happiness. Some patterns are more powerful than others; your daily habits determine your attitude and future progress. So, before you decide to design your success patterns, define how your current practices are helping or hurting you.

### Bad habits are a distraction:

Most people have various kinds of bad habits, like spending too much, lying, or even gossiping. These habits affect productivity and lower the chances of success. To achieve what you want, we need to kill the bad habits that are hurting your progress.

### Habits are the result of your decisions:

Whichever patterns you choose to adopt, it's your decision. So, when you select an excellent habit, think about how it's right for your goals; your habits determine your destiny. If you choose to read inspirational biographies, do it because you linked biographies to your vision.

**Time-management reflects in your habits:**

Whatever your patterns are, they need *time* before they can work. For instance, if you have a habit of watching television for hours, you're trading your time for that habit. Therefore, your good or bad habits affect your time and your long-term success. Think of time as the most valuable currency we can never get back; we're always spending it. Where are you spending yours?

**Developing good habits is in your control:**

It is crucial to remember that only you control the development of your habits. When you adopt patterns that serve you, you'll increase your chances of success. But, you're the only one that can focus your attention on those patterns. Also, wherever your attention goes, you'll get more of that.

# How to build new habits for success

Some habits manifest in your daily life, often as things to do, from brushing your teeth to work; your life's the sum of your habits. The great news is, whatever success you define, the strategies are the same. Your *choices* impact your progress daily. Develop different successful habits with these techniques, and you'll achieve your set goals. Set *clear* and *specific* goals that are important to you. If your goals don't inspire and scare you, you won't reach them; make sure you feel passion for them. Focus on no more than *two* goals, quality over quantity. Having a list of goals is only useful with a tight focus; don't spread yourself thin, and don't multi-task. Describe your goals in detail, so you develop your vision. Vague goals equal vague results. After identifying your *two* goals, add why they're essential to achieve. Many people get bogged down and stop at the start, so get emotional and take advantage of the drive you feel to take action. Now, you're ready to learn practical strategies for developing habits, improving your health, productivity, and achieving your goals.

**Identify the empowering habit you want to adopt:**

First, you need to choose your patterns. Trying to develop ten new habits at the same time will waste your time. Focus on a practice you want to build, and you can always add multiple patterns in the following months, preferably after mastering your first habit. For now, identify a habit you want to develop and write it down. Practices might include: getting up at 5 a.m., for the gym four days a week, reading a book for 30 minutes a day, or journaling at least 1000 words every day. Whatever habits you choose, ensure that you commit to doing them every day; consistency is critical.

**Make a decision:**

Decide to act a specific way 100 percent of the time; your habits are your lifestyle. Let's say you choose to get up early and train every morning. Wear your workout clothes to sleep, set your clock to a specific time, and when the alarm sounds, get up right away and start training. You're not just training to train; you're doing it because you identify as a healthy person.

**Choose the discipline over your mood:**

Imagine if you only trained on the days when you felt fabulous. If your workouts depend on whether you feel blissful, they probably won't be consistent. Decide what actions you plan to take, regardless of your mood. Taking action when you don't feel like it, trains your discipline. You'll be proud to keep your schedule, and this mindset works for any goal. Remember, you can pay the price tomorrow, or you can pay the price today, sooner or later we all pay the price. Your *tomorrow* won't be more comfortable until you decide to *do* today. When you feel like quitting (and we all do), remember your *why* for starting this journey. Remember who you'll be years from now when you breakthrough. This year's going to go by anyway, make it your record year.

**Focus on the big picture:**

One of the main steps in developing lifelong habits is to envision them in your future. In other words, what are your long-term goals? For example, if you want to create a new pattern to write every day, see yourself as a best-selling author. An effective way to focus on the big picture is, to begin with, the end in mind; envision your end goal every day. Studies show that abstract thinking helps you develop the self-discipline to build and maintain new habits. However, there's a caveat. You need to avoid daydreaming and create visualization exercises. Create an *actionable* plan and link it to your internal motivation (your "why"). Your inner motivation is your desire for an intrinsic (rather than an external) reward. A powerful question to ask is, "why do I want to build this new habit?" Think about the reason behind your desire. Once you identify your "why," how can you create more "internal" motivation? When you create your action plan around your "why," you're supporting your new habit.

I used to work with a high-paying real estate company, and one of the first exercises we did was to draw out our "why." The position was commissioned-based, and the average starting income was $150,000 per year. However, the average work hours per week were 80. So, our "why" was critical. This story's remarkable because the people that thrived were always motivated by the things you can't purchase, while the quitters focused on stuff. You knew someone was going to be successful when they concentrated on needs such as love, gratitude, and contribution. However, the unsuccessful always wanted better cars, bigger houses, and more stuff. What feeling are you looking get from your new habit, and what small action will you take to get closer to that feeling? There's no right or wrong answer, just the action that works for you.

**Incorporate the habit with a program:**

After identifying your pattern, create a schedule. This step is crucial because the success of your new practice depends on your commitment to consistency. It's your schedule that will force you to develop the new habit, your tool for accountability. If the pattern you want to establish is reading for 30 minutes per day, what time will you read every day? Similarly, if you're going to exercise in the gym every day, what time do you want it to happen, and for how long? For example, you choose to hit the gym at 6 a.m. and train for an hour. You're setting aside *time* for this objective, and you're dedicating yourself to training every day. Whether you want to train, or don't, you just do it because you commit to yourself.

**Never allow an exception:**

Don't create exceptions to your new pattern. There are no excuses or rationalizations. We need to be able to keep promises to ourselves before anyone else. If you decide to get up at 6 a.m. every day, get up at 6 a.m. every day! You need conscious consistency until it becomes automatic. Create a model of consistency. No one has to remind you to breathe, right? It's automatic. What other patterns can you automate? Maybe it's cardio exercises on Monday, Wednesday, and Friday and strength training on Tuesday and Thursday. Or, take an hour every morning and practice a new social media strategy to promote your business. Find habits that support your goals, and then automate them so you can make steady (daily) progress. Persistence replaces talent, genetics, and luck. There can be no real success without it.

**Get Back Up:**

We have a natural tendency to give up a new habit, especially after we fail to take action or make a mistake. In the early stages of creating a new pattern, your mind will find every possible excuse to leave the ship and return to your old ways. It's even more difficult when your environment doesn't support the change. The more aware you are of the tricks your mind plays, the faster you'll crush them and master your new habit. Be aware that the tendency to stop will occur. Execute the pattern anyway, even if you feel like you're going *through the motions*.

### What is your reward?

At first, people do something because there's a reward, and a habit develops through that cycle. What's the incentive you receive after training in the gym? How would you reward yourself after spending your time reading for 30 minutes a day? If you want to develop a habit, you need the reward. For example, after journaling 1,000-words, grab a snack, rest for a few minutes, or allow yourself to check Instagram. Create something, so your mind knows there's a definite incentive to do the work. Rewards compel people to get into the habit of acting. So, for your daily habits, create little rewards for yourself. After a while, you can replace several smaller prizes with a larger one. For instance, taking a night out to get drinks with friends, monthly trips to the movies, or spa. Spoil yourself; make yourself feel luxurious for your accomplishments.

### Create declarations:

Create statements that you can declare to the world, over and over again. Repeating declarations out loud increases the speed that you'll develop your new habits. For example, you might say, "I'm a champion, I'm changing this world, and I focus on giving" Repeat your declarations before falling asleep. You'll notice that you'll start to become anything you say you are. For added results, say your created statements to yourself in the mirror.

### Track your progress:

When setting your goals, you have a few benchmarks to assess how you're doing. It's easy to get excited about a new target at first. Still, the results depend on the consistency of your actions every day. At the start of a new month, check-in with yourself. Is your plan working? What isn't working? Determine what's working and do more of that, determine what doesn't work, pivot, and drop that action. If an activity doesn't work, it doesn't work. Don't work harder to try to fit a square peg in a round hole. When you regularly track your progress, there's a bonus; you stay connected to your goals. However, you need to be open-minded and fluid, be ready to kill anything that doesn't serve you. The reason why people give up so fast is that they tend to look at how far they still have to go, instead of recognizing the progress they've already made.

**Create success by developing good habits:**

So where do you go from here? Limit your focus to developing one empowering habit every 30 days. The more you try to do, the less you'll achieve. More isn't always more beautiful. It's better to be *all-in* on one project than *half-committed* to ten. Successful people master their actions because they excel at the fundamentals. They focus and exercise the basics every day. Ordinary people, on the other hand, don't see the importance of fundamentals. They look for the next big idea or new trend (shiny objects). That's why people achieve their goals when they practice consistency and discipline. Setting goals isn't something you do once; your goals are living; they need your attention every day. If you want results, start here. Master the fundamentals by developing exceptional habits.

# CHAPTER TWO

## What are *bad* habits?

Bad habits hurt our life. Bad habits can range from careless habits (biting your nails, spinning your hair, checking your phone, spending too much), to full-blown addictions. Addictions are a substitute to meet people's needs. Each of us has six needs: security, variety, love, significance, gratitude, and contribution. Addictions form when a habit meets at least 2 of those needs. The results of our patterns are not instant; some manifest themselves years later, delivering positive or negative consequences. Your habits determine the quality of the life that you live, and bad habits are something that everyone has, nobody is perfect. It's vital to deal with these patterns before they become increasingly difficult to correct. Habits can become addictions or other psychological disorders when there's a lack of willpower. But where there's a will, there's always ways. Everyone has experienced unpleasant habits. Some try to get rid of them; others get rid of them, while the third group of people live with them and just accept them.

Unpleasant habits consist of those habits which don't serve you, don't serve others, and do nothing for the greater good. The most dangerous practices are those learned at a young age. These habits cause considerable damage to human existence, loss of ambition, motivation, premature aging, and various diseases. These unpleasant habits include the consumption of destructive substances: tobacco, alcohol, drugs, toxic and psychotropic substances. There's also less dangerous, but unhealthy habits, such as addiction to computers and smartphones. Diets can be harmful, including weight loss diets and consumption of obesity-causing foods. Also, lack of sleep is dangerous because we need at least 8 hours per day to make effective decisions. Bad habits interrupt your life and prevent you from reaching your goals. They put your health at risk, both mentally and physically. They also waste your time and energy. So why do we have them? And most importantly, what can you do about it?

# Causes of bad habits

Bad habits simply exist because they're meeting a few of our needs at a low-level. Bad habits occur in forms such as nail-biting, over-spending on shopping, drinking every day, and wasting time online. Or bad habits can be a simple response to stress and boredom. It's the things we do without thinking about it that dilute our relationships and stop us from getting what we want. Some habits are harmless but annoying, such as interrupting people. While others are more harmful, such as lying, regardless, you can always *choose* to replace habits, meeting your needs in more fulfilling ways. The following is a practical list of bad habits; repairing these will elevate your quality of life.

**Stress:**

Stress occurs because of expectations, and we only control two elements in our lives. We can manage our thoughts and our actions. When we feel pressure, it's because reality doesn't match the expectation we have. If you thought you'd get a yearly bonus and you didn't, it's stressful. It's stressful because the *hope* of an annual reward doesn't match the *reality* that it didn't occur. Still, what do we do about stress? We can change our *thoughts* and define the situation differently; find what's good about the situation. Or we can improve our environment by moving to a new position, finding a new job, or starting a new business. Change your mind or change your situation; these are your only controls to soothe stress. Below is a list of common reactions to stress.

- **Emotional Eating:**

     Sometimes we go through difficult situations, and food is a crutch for many to cope with stress. If you realize that food is your mechanism for anxiety, it can be a problem that compromises your health, such as gaining weight. Poor self-maintenance causes more stress, compounding our already tricky situation. Coping with emotional consumption causes a poor diet that can lead to blood sugar imbalances and create higher levels of stress. If you have foods and drinks to consume emotionally, remove them from your home; you can't use what you don't have. Also, downsize your plates, bowls, and cups to smaller sizes. The idea is that you'll consume less if the containers are small. You're changing your mind by throwing away *trigger* items, and you're providing support by changing your environment (getting smaller containers).

### ☐ Substances:

Substance abuse is a common habit among stressed people. People can often turn to substances, drugs, smoking, and alcohol to deal with their problems. Let's take a look at drinking, for example. If you are of legal age, occasionally drinking with friends is fine. Still, drinking alcohol every day to deal with stress, causes problems. It's a habit that's meeting several needs. To beat substance abuse, replace the bad habit with an empowering practice that meets the same needs. For example, someone can get high from drugs or get high from jogging. Both methods are attending to the same needs, but jogging is meeting them in an uplifting way.

### ☐ Procrastination:

When you delay doing things on time, you can panic. Panic makes you stress even more because you have more work to do in less time. The best thing you can do is face each task individually, don't multi-task.

Measure how long it will take to complete the work, and just do it! You'll feel less stressed while producing more. Try procrastinating with procrastination. Tell yourself, "I'll procrastinate tomorrow!" This technique works because *tomorrow* never comes.

- **Doing it alone:**

    For some people, independence is an excellent feature because they prefer to rely on themselves. But, consider the power of teamwork; the leverage of multiple people united under one mission. You can try doing it all by yourself, but it's tricky. Getting help from your family, friends, and consultants can end up being a rewarding experience because you're leveraging a team to get what you want.

- **Focusing on mistakes you've made:**

    The sooner you accept the things you can't change, the sooner you stop seeing mistakes as anything but valuable lessons, the better you'll be. An obsession "what if's" (what if I had done **X**) won't change anything, and it's not healthy for your mental state. The only thing you can change is your thoughts and actions. Focus on next time. Stress (pressure) can be positive and push you to the next level. But, stress can be harmful, and bring bad habits into your life; that's when it's time to change. Changing your behavior gets to the root of the problem. Once you *choose* to change your responses to positive ones, you'll improve your habits and be on your way to living a healthier, happier life. Positive stress is a blessing because our strength comes from stressful situations. Don't dwell and don't wish anxiety away; wish for the positive pressure that pushes you to grow.

**Boredom:**

Like stress, boredom leads to bad habits. To deal with boredom, many people begin to waste time watching television or surfing the internet. When we were kids, we were active, and when we were bored, we found something to do with ourselves. As adults, we find ways to fill in the gaps of boredom; to distract ourselves. It's as though we don't want to be alone with our thoughts. In most instances, bad habits are simply a distraction to deal with boredom. Everything from nail-biting, spending too much shopping, drinking, and wasting time online can be distractions for stress and boredom. But it does not have to be this way. You can teach yourself healthy ways to apply your time, overwriting time-wasters with success-makers. Of course, monotony on the surface comes from more deep-seated challenges. It can be challenging to think about these problems. Still, if you are serious about making changes, you must be honest with yourself. Is there a belief or reason behind bad habits? Is there something deeper (a fear, an event, or a limiting belief) that makes you hold on to something that hurts you? Realizing the causes of bad habits is essential to overcoming them.

**Lousy company (peer pressure):**

Many times, bad habits come from our network. If someone is horrible, they'll do their best to enjoy their bad habits. Peer pressure is a real significant factor, and it doesn't go away after high school. Our networks cause tension, which can be positive or negative. Peer pressure is contagious, like the flu, and the people we spend the most time with are the ones creating the influence. Likewise, we influence the people around us. Almost all people from different backgrounds have experienced peer pressure in one way or another. Many understand how negative peer pressure can affect their life, so let's break this down. What are some ideas, habits, or lifestyles that you don't like and don't want to accept? Have you experienced being told what you should do from family or peers? Did you do what they wanted, even though you didn't want to? When we give in to peer pressure, it causes deep pain and remorse because we're not trusting our inner voice. We're burying who we are, for the sake of others.

If four of the five people in your group are millionaires, you're likely to be the fifth. If four of the five people in your group are drug addicts, get ready to be the fifth. You are your network. Always strive to increase your networks' average.

# Bad habits that can jeopardize your success

Habits are unconscious actions that we do in our daily lives. They're part of our identity. We hardly notice them, but they're always present in our gestures, contributing to who we are. There are two main types of habits, let's call them the good guys and the bad guys. The good guys build empires, while the bad guys destroy. It's an internal struggle, and the one that wins is the one you feed. Some bad guys keep us running in circles, never unlocking our potential. They want to keep us in bad routines, never moving towards fulfillment. If left alone, they can permanently sabotage any efforts to improve. It's more important than ever to know who the bad guys are and how to avoid them.

We all have bad guys that we struggle with, but do you let them tear you down? It's not about biting your nails or fidgeting, but the unconscious actions you don't realize. If your goal is to enhance your quality of life, read this list carefully, and identify if you have any of these bad habits. These are the most common bad habits that prevent people from breakthroughs.

**Lazing around:**

I'll write that novel after my favorite T.V. show, after a snack, after a nap, after dinner, tomorrow!" One of the most challenging and apparent parts of achieving success is doing the work. Procrastinating, apologizing, or justifying will only cement the fact that nothing's getting done. Procrastination isn't friends with successful people. Many learn to master procrastination, struggle, and carry on, despite the temptation to park on the couch. It's not pleasant, but the easiest way to accomplish anything is to make *work* your best friend.

**Laziness:**

Laziness paralyzes our desire to succeed. It's that temptation to neglect to produce because of distractions or discomfort; it's taking the "easy" way. Laziness and procrastination go together like peanut butter and jelly. To be successful, you have to work. Don't let this habit rule you; choose to define yourself as an active person. Take a deep breath, count down from 5, and commit to getting the work done.

### Perfectionism:

It has almost become a joke that people think perfectionism is a bad habit. True perfectionism stems from a fear of failure. "Perfectionists" don't want to feel failure, because they don't want to see themselves as a failure. A lot of this mindset comes from traditional schools. In a conventional school, the student is memorizing answers for tests and quizzes. The better they remember the material, the better their grade. So, students try to be "perfect" and get that "perfect" grade. Unlike school, life always gives us the test *first* and the lesson *after*. Successful people understand that success involves a lot of failures, false starts, first drafts, and remakes. People that reach ultra-success are simply people who have failed more than others. Your number of failures will equal your level of success. Fail more, fail often, and don't be fooled into thinking that everything needs to be perfect; it never will be.

### Blaming:

"It's not my fault; I'm not successful because the market's terrible; money's scarce, and the government ruined the economy!" Blaming is useless and destroys your wealth. Remember, we're in an incredible time where people have achieved breakthroughs by launching successful start-ups in their bedroom. Again, nearly everything is out of your control except for thoughts and actions. Blaming others is a waste of those thoughts and actions. There are only three things we can choose to blame in our lives: other people, other things, or ourselves. Don't blame any of those three; take responsibility for your life as it is. You created the life you live, and you can *create* a new one anytime you choose.

**Worrying about what others think and letting it influence your decisions:**

Humans are social animals. We seek acceptance and social interaction. As a result, we care about others' opinions, which destroys our progress. This habit erodes your progress. If you're going to be successful, you must listen to your instincts and trust yourself. You need to be different from the image that your friends, parents, or companies place on you. Only accept what you genuinely believe is right. When you listen to yourself and trust your choices, you develop your unique voice. You grow confidence in your ability to make decisions for yourself. When others push their thoughts on you, you're confident enough to choose your path, for your reasons; you don't seek approval.

**Waiting for opportunities:**

Opportunity doesn't knock on the door for those who sit and wait; they'll miss out. This scenario manifests itself with people waiting for the "easy button" scheme. "If I won the lottery, I would do X, Y, and Z!" As Thomas Edison put it: "Successful people understand that opportunity is fueled by work and putting oneself out there." You can print as many winning lottery tickets as you like by merely seeking opportunities and using your ideas to help enough people get what they want. If money were sticky notes, and you had to collect $1 million of them, what can you produce, that others would trade at least a million sticky notes to have?

**Apologizing for everything:**

Apologizing too much is an unfortunate habit that happens in corporate settings the most. Studies reveal that women are more likely to apologize in the office. By apologizing all the time, you create doubt in your abilities. It makes managers and colleagues lose professional respect for you, limiting upward progress. If you have this terrible habit, stop destroying your future. You have no reason to apologize for your existence. Instead, practice taking full responsibility for yourself and the situation. When you would typically apologize, instead, tell people, "I take responsibility for this, and we'll figure it out."

**Distractions:**

If you find yourself spending more time watching people *live their lives*, than you spend *living your own*, you have a distraction problem. Social media and emails can steal time from us or be productive. You'll find that many successful people turn off notifications and remove distractions from their environment, including apps. The successful choose to abandon these distractions, with the awareness that their time is a *currency* to be spent on critical tasks. We're all given the same 24 hours; nobody can buy more time in a day. If you commit to transforming your life, devote your time to *first things first* and leave distractions at the door. If the action doesn't propel you forward: turn it off, turn it down, delete it, avoid it, delegate it, or automate it. Focus on achieving an environment of silence and solitude with your work.

**Never assume, only anticipate:**

One of the bad habits that stop us is assuming. We can *assume* that our goals are unattainable, our ideas are unacceptable, and other people don't like how we handle specific tasks. Or, you can replace *assumptions* with *anticipation.* Assumptions occur in the absence of information. Therefore, defeat this lousy habit by gathering information before starting. People who are informed *anticipate* needs and desires. Instead of assuming, learn the truth. The unsuccessful are the ones who say, "I *assume* **X**." Assumptions ruin opportunities, and missed opportunities ruin efforts to succeed. People are often amazed at what happens if they take advantage of *learning to anticipate*, instead of assuming they already know. Let's say you work at a spa where your guests need robes and slippers. The unsuccessful attendant makes *assumptions*, choosing the guest's slipper size for them. Can you imagine *assuming* a woman is a size eight slipper when she's a size six? Or, giving someone an XXL robe when they're only a large? Instead, the attendant that anticipates knows the guest will need a robe and slippers. They don't assume the clothing sizes, but they stay ahead of the clients' needs because they've learned what their clients demand. This subtle difference creates massive success. *Anticipate*, don't *assume*.

**Allowing others to set the agenda:**

Not having your priorities straight or putting your preferences behind someone else is one of the worst habits of the unsuccessful. Of course, execute your work, help family and friends, and serve others (these are things everyone should do), but understand where their priorities fit. Successful people are those who dare to say *no thank you* when they don't have the time. Guard your time against time wasters. When others are loose with their time, be disciplined. Just like money, ask yourself if that 4-hour event at the bar is worth spending 4 hours you'll never have again. If people start to say they haven't seen you lately, you're on the right track. If you're so focused that you have to ask someone what day it is, you're on the right track. Your friends may not see you at the bar, but you won't see them at the bank. We all have to pay the price in time and money. The difference is when we choose to pay that price. Pay the price now, so you can be completely free and pay any price later. Ordinary people want to go out, distract themselves. Those people pay the price later on by having to work and scramble for money in old age. Be the person who puts the work in upfront, and spend the rest of your life free, wealthy, and doing whatever you want.

**Resisting change:**

Regardless of your age, if you're reluctant to adopt new technologies, learn new skills, or try new ideas, you'll be left behind. Today the world is moving and changing faster than ever, and those who refuse to change will go down with their ship. However, successful people are open to learning and experimenting. They exercise discipline, not acting on every shiny object they see. The successful are open to new possibilities, and education, they're willing to choose different paths. When we stop growing, we start dying. Don't buy the advice that you can't teach an old dog new tricks; if that dog didn't want to learn anything new, it was on its last leg anyway. Be fluid and accept that *change* is inevitable.

### Liking your work, not loving it:

When you like your work, it tempts you into a comfort zone. It provides you with what you need and doesn't challenge you to grow. You do enough to get by, but your skill level doesn't increase since it's easy to float along. Getting stuck in a comfort zone is a habit that prevents many from achieving success. To become exceptional, you must love your work, take risks, and challenge yourself. The challenge forces you to raise your game. It's been my experience that life is hard for people who choose the easy way. But life is easy for people who commit to the hard way. Would you trade your money for something that you just liked? That was just ok? You'll never get your time back, why would you devote such a valuable resource to something you don't love? If your life's work is important enough for your time, give the majority of your time to what you love! Don't settle for anything less.

# How to get rid of bad habits

Habits are challenging to break because constant repetition creates deep links in our brains. The patterns get reinforced when you add pleasure to them. Our practices are just patterns of behavior, and breaking those behavior patterns is the key to breaking our poor practices. Usually, there's an obvious trigger that starts the model. Triggers are personal, situational, or environmental. For example, if you eat in front of the T.V. when you get home. Your brain connects the dots, and you unconsciously form a connection between T.V. and eating.

One of the most significant issues with bad habits is the physiological change that occurs in your body. This change applies to anyone with a physical addiction—smoking, overeating, excessive alcohol consumption, drugs, and pills. When a material change occurs in the body, we must overcome mental, physical, and emotional obstacles. If the human body is physically dependent on something, breaking it requires much more effort. We need to understand more than psychology to remove bad habits. It's about addressing a physiological change in the body, which is more complicated. We (humans) are not perfect. We know what to do, exercise, eat well, sleep, but we don't always do what we know. Sometimes, what starts as an oversight, coping mechanism, or accident, becomes a bad habit. The great news is that it's possible to eliminate bad habits, and this is how:

### Identify the triggers:

The fridge could be a trigger for you when you get home, just like eating junk food when bored. By identifying your triggers, you can choose new behaviors that meet the same needs more healthily. But some people have a hard time executing it. If you're having a hard time knowing what drives you emotionally, work backward. When you experience a trigger, slow down, be present, and ask yourself, "what emotion am I feeling? The behavior is meeting some of the six needs we all have. They are safety, variety, love, purpose, growth, and contribution. Which of these needs is your behavior meeting? If you had to choose a new action, what could you pick to replace your bad habit, while still meeting your needs?

**Illuminate Your Bad Habit:**

One of the ways to get rid of your bad habit is to illuminate it to your mind. Often our brains work against us getting what we want. To remove that part of the process from the subconscious mind, we must illuminate our bad habits. When we don't bring our bad behaviors to the conscious mind, it's easy for the brain to stay unconscious, never allowing us the opportunity to change. To illuminate our bad habits, write down all of its details. What's a bad habit you want to change? When did it start for you? How did it start? What noticeable effect has it had on your life? Although it's sometimes difficult to admit our weaknesses, it's an essential part of eliminating the habit. The more focus you give your patterns, the easier it will be to replace the ones that don't elevate you.

**Tell your friends and family:**

When you want to accomplish anything, tell your network! And, ask them to keep you accountable. Accountability creates social pressure to fulfill your promise; to do what you said you'll do. Ask supportive people to hold you to your word. Don't request accountability from negative people because their harmful personalities make things more complicated. These people can't hold you accountable because they don't hold themselves responsible for their poor attitudes.

The people around us have a surprisingly significant impact on our behavior. Studies suggest that the risk of obesity increases by 57 percent, for those who have a close friend whose obese, even if the friend lives hundreds of miles away. Other research has suggested that we tend to feel the same way, and adopt the same goals as the people we spend the most time around. So, one way to significantly increase your chances of success is to make sure you have the right people in your corner. If you want to create healthy habits, but your friends don't, it's time to make new friends. And if you're going to make great things happen in your life, you can't be surrounded by pessimists. It's time to create a support group that inspires you; elevates you when you're down. You are the average of the five people you spend the most time with, so be selective, and always increase your standards.

**Go slow and make small changes:**

Forming empowering habits takes effort and time, but breaking established bad habits can be even harder. Be patient with yourself, instead of making dramatic changes focus on one practice. Choose the smallest step you can take to progress. The size of your action is less important than consistency. With food and diet, for example, remove a sugar packet or change the cream to low-fat. Little steps add up to significant results over time, inspiring more remarkable changes.

**Develop a replacement plan:**

Breaking habits isn't about stopping, but substituting. You're replacing *low-level* habits with *more* fulfilling behavior patterns. Your new practice must meet your needs at a high level. For example, you can replace coffee with water, get sugar from fruit instead of candy, and get up early in the morning instead of going to bed early in the morning. The critical point is to prepare a response against your usual triggers.

**Find a strong enough reason:**

In setting goals, you need a purpose that grips your heart so powerful it wakes you up at night. You need the ideas first, and the answers second. When you have compelling reasons, you can accomplish anything. But how many of us fail to find in-depth and compelling reasons? We don't want to be fit just to look good. We want the *feelings* that come with being healthy. We want to *feel* energetic enough to play with our children. We need deep, not fragile, reasons. Find why you have to give up your bad habits, and you'll see your life explode with possibility. To uncover your deep "why," use the seven why's exercise.

1. Why do you want _____in your life?

2. Why do you want (answer to question #1)?

3. Why do you want (answer to question #2)?

4. Why do you want (answer to question #3)?

5. Why do you want (answer to question #4)?

6. Why do you want (answer to question #5)?

7. Why do you want (answer to question #6)?

Write your answers, and don't leave them on your mind. What deep reasons come to mind? Let's say you replace a "bad" habit with an empowering one; often, the old practice will have a more powerful biological "reward" than the new one. You have the power to redefine yourself.

New year's resolutions are ridiculous for this reason. How many people set them, and fall back to their old habits? It's because permanent change isn't a resolution; it's a lifestyle. Who do you think will go to the gym more: the person taking the 30-day challenge, or the person who links their identity to being healthy? The people who label themselves as "healthy" because they work hard to stay congruent with their identity. Do you want more money? It's a great goal, and you need a profound reason for it. You don't care about the cash, but you desire what it does for you. For example, money brings you freedom, security, and the ability to take care of your family (you have deeper reasons).

**Who will you become in five and ten years?**

Imagine your future self, vividly. Where are you going? Towards colossal debt, a heart attack, acute illness? Are there severe restrictions in your future? Are you heading towards destruction if you don't make a change? Now, imagine your future when you make a positive change. How much will your life enrich in five years? Ten years? See the beauty of your new life in your mind. Remind yourself of the positive consequences of changing by writing them down. Review them whenever you feel like quitting and going back to your old ways.

**Change your environment:**

Over time, if you perform the same behaviors, in the same way, the situation becomes a trigger (sometimes too subtle to be noticed). Change your environment in any small way, and you'll support your changed behavior. The 20-second rule helps: make bad habits waste 20 extra seconds. For example, you need to inconvenience yourself when you want to act on poor practices. Want to watch T.V.? Put the remotes in another room on a high shelf. Force yourself to get a step stool and walk into another room to get them. Are you concerned with your credit card use? Put all of your credit cards in a lockbox. Force yourself to have to get the key and consciously retrieve them. In these scenarios, you use inconvenience to your advantage.

**Support and reward yourself:**

When breaking a habit, you get to a point where you want to stop trying. You ask yourself, "why am I fighting this?" You feel discouraged, thinking that you are making your life more stressful for fewer rewards. It happens to us all; it's the lowest point in the process, where you need to reflect on why you're changing. You need to create a reward system for yourself, for instance, celebrating yourself with a special dinner, before jumping into the next goal. How will you spoil yourself? You deserve to feel luxurious and pamper yourself for your accomplishments.

Again, always surround yourself with people who encourage you, support you, understand you and keep you on track.

**Track and analyze:**

Quitting a bad habit is similar to other goals. To accomplish what you've decided to do, you need to track and analyze it. The more detailed you keep track of things, the more likely you are to win. For example, if you are trying to stop consuming foods or drinks with excessive amounts of sugar or fat, wouldn't you monitor your results daily? What are the feelings associated with the behavior? By tracking, we can observe our progress. Use the "small" start approach to eliminate misbehavior over time. Use a notepad, smartphone, or spreadsheet program on your desktop or tablet as a tracking system and analyze your results daily. No matter how you choose to proceed, select your tracking system and stick to it. Keep in mind that it takes 18-254 days to create lasting habits (with an average of 66 days). This timeframe also applies to bad habits. Don't be discouraged if it doesn't happen overnight. Give yourself room to breathe, stay persistent, and monitor your results over time. I prefer to use stickk.com to set up and track my progress. It's a phenomenal tool for tracking, analyzing, community, and accountability.

**Stay persistent:**

Persistence is the art of not giving up. It takes a lot to be persistent with our goals, whatever they may be. And giving up bad habits is no different. Let's say you find yourself stumbling, or repeatedly failing, Do you get up and keep going? The time's going to pass by anyway, quitting guarantees nothing happens. By merely trying again, you've automatically increased your chance of success.

Have you ever noticed that nobody gets worse with practice? Each time we show up, we improve. We also alter our neurochemicals, neural pathways, and our physiology. Like anything else that's worthwhile, it's not easy. Giving up your bad habits takes effort, which is why we must need a network of like-minded people on the same journey. If problems persist, find a mentor. Find someone whose given up the same bad habit you want to remove, ask for their advice, and trust their guidance when you need it. How do you know if someone can guide you? Here's the test, have they lived what they're telling you? If they've lived their advice, they know it. Can the poor tell you how to make millions of dollars? No, because they haven't *lived* it. If they had, they'd have millions of dollars. How often do we get advice from people who haven't *lived* the information they're giving? It happens all the time! Remember, a person *knows it* if they've *lived it*.

Stay persistent, stay hungry, know that there will be a lag time to see results, and remember that time will go by anyway; use that time to create your dream life!

**Do not make a huge deal out of it:**

If you think about a habit you don't like and talk about it all the time, you'll make it bigger than it deserves. That's not to say you're facing a little challenge, but your problems are only as big as the attention you give them. Focusing on what we don't like is mentally taxing and makes us feel overwhelmed. Keep it simple and keep in mind that whatever pattern you want to remove, thousands, if not millions, have done it before. Yes, things get tricky from time to time. But giving our problems too much attention complicates them. Have you ever noticed when you want something, it seems to show up everywhere? You never saw it before, but now that you desire it, it seems to find you in everything you do. Our challenges are the same way. Imagine you're rafting, and there's a fallen tree in the water. If you focus on what you want to avoid (the fallen tree), you're highly likely to hit it. Instead, focus on where you're going. Life is the same way. Be aware that there's a "fallen tree" (your problem) and paddle with everything you have towards where you want to go (your goals).

# CHAPTER THREE

## What is success?

Tony Robbins said: "Success without fulfillment is the ultimate failure." Achieving success means achieving a life that makes you feel significant. A critical component to success is defining your version of it; there's no universal success, only individual. The real meaning of success goes far beyond standard definitions, such as wealth, cars, and homes. Instead, real achievement comes from *how many* (width) people you serve and how deeply (depth) you serve them. It's not the trophies we collect, although the media and society measure success by those means. Extraordinary riches and lavish things don't measure success. But, success is a life well-lived, a sense of satisfaction knowing that the world is more remarkable because of you.

Do you want to crank out that kind of success? You need to tap into your genius zone.

How do we harness our inner-brilliance? By doing what inspires you, and finding ways to use your inspiration to make other people successful. When you help enough people get what they want, you get the freedom, lifestyle, and experiences you want. Success, too, can be defined by who you are and the person you aspire to be. Success is different for every person, and it's as diverse as the human race. A small achievement for one person can be a milestone for another. Someone once told me to treat all your victories in the same way, however small they may seem. In today's society, people compare their achievements to others. Still, the goals they set come through hard work and grit. Be proud of what you do so that no one can undermine your goals and dreams. Every time you reach a new milestone, you should be thankful that you're one step closer to a massive breakthrough. We all want to be successful, and we're all more than capable of achieving it. Our *contributions* define success, and contributing to others is where you tap into the purpose and motivation to overcome any obstacles ahead.

# Characteristics of successful people

Do you want to feel accomplished in your life? Did you know it's as simple as modeling the people who have what you want? However, you need to model the right skills and characteristics. As the gardener of your life, you choose what skills and attributes go in your garden; it's vital to cultivate yourself this way for the best yield. Nobody wakes up, accidentally successful. The results occur because of daily habits. Remember: if you live your life like most people, you'll get what most people get. You don't want what most people have, do you? No! Don't you want freedom and choices? Yes! You'll enjoy the "fruits" when you improve your "roots."

Success is not a single quality, characteristic, or trait. Everyone would be successful if it were a handout. Instead, success is a delicate blended mix of your characteristics and habits. Just like ingredients in a meal, too much confidence, or too little attention to detail, will cause the dish to fall apart. Everyone wants success; nobody's passion is to become a lousy business owner. However, what separates the average from the best? Traits and behaviors. Identifying them is easy; practicing them is the challenge. Below are the attributes to practice now:

### Confidence:

When we cultivate confidence, everything seems more natural; we act with greater conviction and passion. You work hard, you produce, and have a sense of inner-strength. You're proud to complete work, and you take responsibility when necessary. Your confidence guides your purpose, and you associate your identity with excellence. Self-confidence is essential and grows with action (success breeds more success). The person with the least mistakes, failures, and insults is usually the safest in the room. In staying safe, these people remain mediocre and unfulfilled. Our comfort zone is a success crusher! However, the *larger* our comfort zone is, the *larger* our wealth zone is. Whether you're starting your journey or ready to crank it to the next level, remember: it will never be perfect. Still, experts reduce their risks significantly and are more confident and assured.

Experts have the knowledge to back up their victories because they aggressively grow themselves. There's no magic pill for success, but there are a few "vitamins" you should take. Educate yourself, always give more than expected, and fail often. To be the one that stands out, realize that your greatest asset is you—everything changes when you stop "chasing" success and grow to become the person who attracts it.

## Communication:

The most effective communicators want to be the most *interested,* instead of trying to be the most *interesting*. People help people that they like, and people enjoy others that are like them. When you're the most *interested* in other people, they can't help but appreciate you. When they feel understood by you, they want to do more for you. Communication is about 80% non-verbal, and you should only be speaking 20% of the time. When you exercise that 20%, you need to express interest and ask other people questions. While people talk, observe their body language, and mirror it subtly (people like people that are like them, including body language). Effective communication produces trust and respect. You're not mediocre; you have a communication plan. Mediocrity occurs when you don't plan. If you want to get what you want, you need people. These are the behaviors that will get people on your side and get you what you want. Model successful behavior every day. When you act with grace, courage, and faith, you become fearless. That's who you really are, who you have always been.

## Network:

Successful people are aware that the people they spend time with have a significant influence on who they become. Successful people want to spend time with people who advance their lives. Being around these people encourages them to make the most of their gifts and skills. Understand, elite people always guard their elite network. One of your goals is to grow the average of your core group as you develop yourself; you're reaching up. When you reach up, you'll need to demonstrate the value you bring to other people. Don't expect to be let into their core group easily; you'll be replacing someone else in their inner circle. The best way to reach up to new networks is to figure out how to serve the people in those networks. Your goal is to demonstrate that you want to bring value to people and learn from them. There's nothing valuable about someone who thinks they already know everything. Find out what you can do for others, be open-minded, and approach networking with a service mindset. Lastly, choose to network with groups of people that scare you. Reach up to a level where the people make you feel intimidated.

There's no growth in being a big fish in the little pond.

**Ambition:**

Ambitious people have visions of their best selves; they think big. If you feel inferior, like you're a victim, you won't reach your goals. There's no such thing as a successful victim. You need to give *everything to everything*. Redefine yourself as a person that leaves everything on the field. When you do anything, play full-out! That way, you can take comfort in knowing it's not your fault you failed, you did everything in your control. We all experience setbacks out of our control! But that doesn't mean we curl up and stop—the same amount of energy is required to be ambitious as it is to be fearful. So, permit your desires to pull you, and don't resist. If you know what you want to achieve and commit to being ambitious; This will help you.

**Positivity:**

Harv Eker, the author of The Secrets Of The Millionaire Mind, said, "how you do anything is how you do everything." Positivity is a choice. Negativity is a choice. Life doesn't *happen* to us; life is neutral, and we choose what everything means.

Every day, you can define everything as positive or negative, either way, you're right. Whichever one you decide is what you'll feel. Your emotions will determine how you act and how you act will produce your result. Your result will be positive or negative, depending on how you were thinking. Now you know you can think positively and get positive results. You know it doesn't take any additional energy to think positively or negatively. So, what's the point of choosing negative responses? There is none. Positive results await you as soon as you *decide* to define yourself as a positive person. Just change your mind; it's that simple. When you see the positive in everything, your life will reflect those thoughts.

Alternatively, cynical characters are pessimistic in other parts of life. You probably know (and work with) both types of people. The critical component of a positive person is their ability to consider a challenge and say, "we'll figure it out." Positive people acknowledge they don't have all the answers, but they still don't quit. They'll figure it out. The crucial differences in a negative person are that they'll face the same problem, and complain about it, blame something else, or justify it. That's why positive personalities are assets for every team. They're willing to learn, adapt, and "figure out" challenges. Remember, everything in life is neutral; you choose the definition. Choose to become a positive force.

**Organization:**

Successful people stay organized. You'll rarely find someone successful who throws the organization into the wind with their daily activities. That's why it's essential to use technology to your advantage. Download apps that automate work and centralize your operations. For example, an email client that organizes all your emails in one place. Activity management apps like Asana, Trello, or Teamwork help you keep your team on the same page, your tasks completed on time, and your projects on track.

**Successful people take care of themselves:**

Successful people realize they can only *offer* their best when they're already *at* their best. You can't be the best without taking care; eating healthy foods, getting enough rest, and exercising. As a result, you feel better and look better, increasing self-esteem. Activities outside of work are vital; What hobbies do you love? Who do you adore that would appreciate more of your time? Who makes you feel good about yourself? Taking care of yourself means tending to your fulfillment.

**Courage:**

Most people don't succeed because of fear. Many people are afraid of failing, and some are even afraid of success. These irrational fears prevent them from achieving what they want. However, the most successful people agree that failure's critical for success; mistakes are necessary. You need this mindset! You need courage.

Do this: First, imagine the most significant fears holding you back from the success you want. Second, I want you to write them down. Whatever crazy thoughts come to your mind, write them. Third, look at what you wrote; these are your extremes. Fourth, write down what you'll still have if all of your fears occurred. You'll realize that what you imagine isn't as bad as you think. You'll survive, you'll thrive, and you'll always be able to express gratitude for your life.

Setbacks are the lessons necessary for learning and growth. Without challenges, everyone would be successful, and it would be meaningless. We owe life's challenges a *thank you*, for stopping weak, undeserving people from taking your success. Courage means acknowledging fear exists and pushing forward anyway; it's a great feature to have if you want results. We all have anxiety and doubts, but we can all choose to act regardless. Acting even though fear exists is the champion's way. Since you've read this far, that's you.

### Responsibility:

It's a sign of strength and maturity. People who stand up and admit they made a mistake, prove it with their behavior. Accountability is critical because it keeps people honest. Self-responsibility is a rare quality because someone willing to accept they've failed will be ready to learn from your failure. But people who blame cause problems. They're the people who don't take responsibility for what happened. Insecure people want to blame someone, something, or themselves. They're happy to "throw someone under the bus" if it gets the attention off of them. This unfortunate behavior causes challenging work relationships with other people. People who accept responsibility make life easier for those around them, they learn more and achieve.

### Live for something bigger than yourself:

Do you believe in a higher power, have a strong belief in family values, love for your country, or your peers? Successful people know their actions are significant. Living for something beyond ourselves, magnifies our sense of purpose. Steve

Jobs put a "dent in the universe "when he envisioned the iPod, iPad, and iPhone. What dreams do you have? Your thoughts need to be so colossal that you're in awe of your purpose. Pay attention to your mission, and you'll notice it touches other people; you're never the only person that will benefit. How will you benefit humanity? Which of your gifts will you use to leave this world more exceptional than you found it? You're not on this planet to pay bills and die; you're here to fulfill a mission. You're here for a reason, and while I don't know you, I know you have ideas that will benefit us all. Don't hide your brilliance from me or the rest of the world.

**Commitment:**

Are you familiar with the difference between affirming and declaring? The difference is commitment. There's a reason the United States didn't call it the "affirmation" of independence. Affirmation is telling ourselves something over and over until we believe it. Can you imagine if the United States had sat around telling themselves, "we're a free people!" The United States could have kept telling themselves they were free, but it wouldn't have made it real, and the British would have imposed their will. Instead, the U.S. created the "*Declaration* of Independence" This document *declared* to Britain that the United States is a nation of free people, by *declaring* war. Can you see the critical difference? When the U.S. *declared* war, they committed. Your success will come from your commitment. Don't affirm that you're going to be successful, people who do are just convincing themselves they're something that they're not. Declare your intention-your commitment-to reach the heights of success on your terms.

**Resilience:**

Life always pushes back right before a breakthrough. When you experience adversity, you're only inches away from getting what you want. How often have we stopped moments before achieving our goal? Resilience is a crucial characteristic. It helps you push past the limits you set for yourself. You'll face obstacles, challenges, and things that detour your success. Resilience is the "bounce" you have when the ball drops. If you're not resilient, just like a basketball with no air, you can't bounce. Our resolve gets tested when faced with situations that don't go as *expected*. Everyone can be great when times are excellent. However, resilient people are still exceptional when things are crashing around them. You expand your resilience by not creating expectations and keeping your mind fluid. Don't set yourself in stone, always be ready to adapt, and you'll overcome, and thrive. That's easier said because *believing* you have the power to bounce back is difficult. Primarily when everything in your environment is pointing to failure. Still, resilience is a behavior that exists to benefit you. You can have anything you want from life if your ability to "bounce back" is more persistent than life's tests.

# Your successful habits list

What if you could adopt the exact behaviors of the people who have the success you want? Modeling is a well-researched way to learn. The list of successful habits below will give you everything you need to get what you want by modeling others who already have it. It includes elements we can use every day to be more productive. In addition to skills, intelligence, and opportunities, these habits will make a difference for you. People reach pinnacles of success because they regularly practice specific habits that work, habits that ordinary people don't use.

Most people go through life, jealous of the success of others, unaware of the failures and hard work that came with it. These people feel insecure about where they are because they compare their life (apples) to someone else (oranges). Many never know that they can have the same success if they just model what the other person does. Developing new habits requires diligence, discipline, and commitment to follow a plan for at least 60-90 days. Even though 90 days is a grain of sand over the life of a person, many don't commit. The secret is to start *small* and choose one or two habits as your focus. Once those habits are ingrained, you can add more patterns later in the year.

Here's a list of the most powerful practices that successful people incorporate into their lives. When you commit to starting these behaviors, and making them an integral part of your life, your potential is infinite:

**Routines:**

We need structure and routine in our lives; our bodies expect it. They work best when we operate routinely, and above all, we need to eat and sleep at the same time every day. If you're the parent of a young child, you know to teach this habit early. Routines remain with a person for life and help them develop outstanding work habits. Find a schedule that's right for you and stick with it. Start by setting timers on your phone to go off every day for an early morning wake up, breakfast, pausing for a moment of silence and gratitude, lunch, dinner, and bedtime.

**Relaxation:**

Relaxing by meditation and avoiding distractions is another prominent habit of successful people. Seek the places that provide the most silence. Silence does incredible wonders for the mind because when the noise goes away, serenity begins. *Quiet* is the most significant benefit of waking up early. The calm promotes relaxation, and relaxation supports clear thinking. Many people don't wake up early, and it's astounding how still the Earth is in the early morning. Of course, relaxation is also more natural for organized people; a cluttered space creates a cluttered mind. Next, "breathing" is how successful people center themselves. Focus on deep breathing for 3-5 minutes, at the start of your morning, to achieve a balanced state. Breathe deep and exhale. Lastly, change your physiology; if you're sitting stand, and if you're standing walk. When you change your physiology (body), you're changing your emotions instantly.

**Create your luck:**

Successful people understand that luck comes from the preparation and work; they're proactive about *creating* their future. Entrepreneurs choose to make their fortune rather than wait for someone to make it for them. Microsoft, Apple, Facebook, and Lululemon all exist because visionaries built them from scratch. It's funny, so many people's retirement plan is to win the lottery. However, the harder we work towards our life-purpose, the more "luck" we create. Luck isn't about a chance happening; it happens when people put in the effort and are prepared to take advantage of opportunities that present themselves. Look at real estate, for example, the housing market crash in 2008 was very *unlucky* for most (the unprepared). Still, it was *lucky* for real estate investors.

Contrary to the media's doom and gloom, the entire housing market went on sale. The investors who prepared (had cash reserves) and worked hard (acquired real estate knowledge and experience ) were *lucky*. Their *fortune* came from that hard work and preparation. Luck is not out of your control, because preparing and putting forth effort is not out of your control. Use this knowledge to create your fortune.

**Measure success in happiness instead of money:**

The modern generation of employees is increasingly motivated by money, job satisfaction, and benefits. This shift represents a change in the way people measure success. Defining it in pounds, pence, dollars, and cents never leads to true fulfillment. Thinking in terms of money will backfire. So, create a clearly defined vision of what success means to you and determine what'll fulfill you. Write it down. Start by observing what you'd *prefer* to be doing with your time. Measure your success by the quantity of time you give, each day, to the things that energize you. Let's say John works 40 hours a week at a job he doesn't really like, making $100,000 per year.

John loves fishing and goes out every weekend for 20 hours. Now, let's say Dana works 20 hours a week at a job she doesn't really like, and makes $50,000 per year. Dana loves dancing and goes five days a week for 40 hours. Who's more successful? John doubles Dana's income, so he should be happier right? But, Dana has twice as much free time doing what she loves. For most people, they'd rather be in Dana's shoes than John's. I challenge you to increase your time per week, doing what you love while reducing your time doing the things you don't. You need to take the items you don't like and automate them, eliminate them, or delegate them. You're playing to increase your time doing what you love, while simultaneously improving your income. It's possible, and it's critical. Measure your happiness in time, not money.

**Live a healthy life:**

Our brains need the right type of food to perform at their best. Don't operate on an empty stomach. Train yourself to follow a balanced and healthy diet. We tend to maintain the habits we learn when we're young for most of our lives. Learning how to eat can prevent many health problems along the way. Successful people understand the importance of diet, exercise, and hygiene. For some, personal care involves complex routines and a highly disciplined lifestyle. For others, not so much. Elon Musk, CEO of Tesla Motors, was asked what daily habit has the most significant [positive] impact on your life? To this, Musk simply said, "Showering." Successful people take care of themselves! Managing stress and staying mentally sharp helps them excel every day. Whether meditation, breakfast, or gym time, successful people know that physical and mental well-being is a priority.

Taking care of yourself shows you value yourself, and your performance increases. When you run a business, work is stressful, or you're focused on growing your family, it's easy to let physical and mental well-being slip. However, in the long run, you'll be better at everything you do when you're healthy. Ponder these questions, would you want millions of dollars if you weren't fit enough to leave your home? Would you want the biggest mansion in Malibu if all you could do is lay in bed? Fame, fortune, and things mean nothing if you're not healthy enough to enjoy life. Sacrificing health for wealth is a massive failure. Take care of your health, so you can take care of your wealth and live the fulfilling life you deserve with the people you cherish.

**Don't be afraid to take risks (or fail!):**

Taking risks is one of the essential habits of successful people. Doesn't it endanger your dreams? There's no reward without risk. By not taking risks, you're still taking a chance on your future. When you take risks, if you do what everyone else is doing, you'll get what everyone else has. The most significant journey begins when you act differently; when you leave your comfort zone. Abandoning what's comfortable forces you to push your limits and innovate. Successful people take *educated* risks to move forward. However, remember this, every chance in life isn't good or bad; it's the risk-taker that's good or bad. The situation is good or bad based on the skill and education of the person taking the risk. If you've never been sky diving, would you jump by yourself the first time? I hope not! However, for the people who have done thousands of jumps, it's just another day at the "office." Skill, education, and control determine the level of the risk. Failure is part of life; don't be discouraged. Instead, use it as a learning experience. Find out what went wrong, avoid repeating the error next time, and you'll avoid the same result.

**Challenge yourself and do difficult things:**

You can't be successful in life without personal growth. Progress requires a willingness to accept and overcome difficult challenges. It's only through overcoming obstacles that we can learn and develop critical life skills, and it's these attributes that will bring success. By challenging yourself and facing difficult tasks, you change your mindset about life's possibilities. When we take the easy route, life gets complicated. The secret to making life easy is to do difficult things. The added benefit of taking the difficult way is that it's much less crowded. For example, have you ever seen a Social Security office? There's one up the road from us in Hawaii, and it's jammed with people from open to close. Up the road from that is a financial complex that looks like a ghost town. The point is, trying to live on Social Security makes for a hard life. But, investing every extra dollar, saying no to things that don't serve your future, and paying the price now, creates your wealth (the easy life).

**Practice gratitude:**

It's effortless to have a bad habit of envying what others have. The grass often looks greener on the other side. It's vitally important to learn gratitude. Practice finding gratitude in everything. Let's take a few minutes now; what can you be grateful for right now? I'm thankful for you. Choose anything around you and express gratitude. You'll always receive *more* of what you appreciate. Try this, set the alarm on your phone to go off 1-3 times a day, to say, "Be grateful." You can choose morning, afternoon, and evening to set the alerts. When they go off, stop everything you're doing, take a deep breath, and express what you're thankful for out loud. You're practicing conscious gratitude, which will soon become an unconscious pattern.

**Develop good learning habits:**

Effective studying is a skill. Individuals who live life to the fullest are lifelong learners; They never stop trying new things. It's necessary to research and gather new knowledge effectively and efficiently. Learning to study and gain experience to succeed isn't natural; you learn how to learn. To improve your study habits, take a study skills course, or ask others who are where you want to be. However, don't get caught in the "learning trap." Many people learn but never take action. What I'm talking about is learning just to learn. These are the people who use education to mask their fear of doing. In college, there was a presentation on marketing; each student got up and "taught" a topic. The topics ranged from "how to go viral on social media," to "effectively marketing your e-commerce store with Google ads." It was ridiculous because it occurred to me that these students only knew what they read. How can you teach me how to go viral when you have a following of a couple hundred friends and family? Why are we learning google ads from a person who never put up their money to advertise? People can learn anything, but it doesn't qualify them to perform it. You'd never get heart surgery from a person who just read all about it, would you? You want to know the person has *done* it, that they *live* it. Always be learning, but make sure you *practice*. Education *without* experience is just information; knowledge *with* experience creates wisdom.

**Set high goals:**

Everyone knows that goals are essential. Without a clear purpose, life and business have no direction. In the case of running a business, successful people quantify and measure success. If they're not reaching their goals, they don't let them go; they brainstorm how to change what doesn't work. Successful people not only create goals but micro-objectives. Some goals will be immediate; some are short-term; some are to reach a specific target, or complete a particular project. Others will be more ambitious and long-term, such as expanding into a new market. Write all your goals down and review them regularly to make sure you're moving in the right direction. Also, write out a "not-to-do" list. Often, people have a list of things to get done. But, it's rare when people create a list of things never to do. The purpose of your "not-to-do" list is to write everything that takes you away from your goals. For instance, if you spent three hours grocery shopping, put it on the list. Once you have your list of things never to do, decide if you can eliminate it, delegate it to someone else, or make it automatic. For the previous example, have you ever used Instacart? It's a grocery delivery app.

You choose groceries from your phone and hire a person to shop for them for you. Imagine if you had someone who gets your groceries while you work at home, creating an asset that pays you money. You pay the Instacart shopper a $20 tip, while you use your time to generate $100 in profit. Set a lofty goal, create a list of anything that doesn't serve your purpose, and decide how to handle those distractions.

**Visualize Success:**

Successful people aim to dominate, and this includes visualizing. Whether meditation or other means, visualization's a powerful mechanism! Many high-achievers plan and write their goals early in the morning, setting the tone for the day. This simple action prepares the mind for achievement; studies show that visualization works. You're training your brain to think in achievement mode. Your days will flow according to your mindset in the morning. If you visualize dominating your habits every day, your feelings, actions, and results will obey.

Now that you understand the power of positive visualization to change behaviors. Most research shows that merely visualizing change isn't enough to maintain habits. Researchers found that people taught *how* to improve their patterns, most likely will. For example, instead of memorizing a new language, those living in the culture, practicing it every day, are more likely to become fluent. Don't visualize yourself after you've mastered your new pattern. Instead, imagine yourself practicing the habit every day. The consistency of the activity, every day, is more important than the result.

**Learn from Failure:**

Failure is a teacher of valuable life lessons; make failure meaningful by reflecting on painful experiences. What lessons can you learn from each failure? Every experience has gems of wisdom in them. It's your job to find them and apply them in the pursuit of your breakthroughs. By addressing the issue directly and identifying exactly where things went wrong, you can avoid the same mistakes. Different actions create different results, which create failures that vary. When failures change, what you learn changes. This process of change enables you to improve your decisions, which improves your actions, improving your results.

# CHAPTER FOUR

## Training your mind to stick to your new habit

If you've ever tried to reach an ambitious goal, you're probably familiar with how difficult it is to change your habits. You're aware of how much influence your mind has in determining your success. However, you've experienced results that aren't consistent (we all have). Your brain corresponds to your body and actions. Habits are primarily the product of deep-seated pathways in the brain, linked to your environment. When you get in the car, for example, you buckle up because of the familiar sights and sounds or get set up the same way every time. There was a time in the past when these actions were conscious; you thought about them and made the decisions. But now they're automatic. Research has found that circuits in the brain that control habits can effectively compete with circuits that control conscious actions. To create a new pattern, you need to repeat the same behavior in a consistent environment. This element is crucial. You're anchoring your new habit to a specific environmental cue. For example, you practice your new pattern when you're stuck in traffic or right after cleaning the dishes at night. What's your signal? It's short. If you're trying to read more books, for example, anchor it by reading while the dishwasher's going. Or, listen to audiobooks in your car while you're in traffic. Research has shown that these repeated behaviors form habits using multiple regions of the brain.

With a little initial discipline, you can create a new habit that requires little effort to maintain. Here are some tips for forming new habits and making them stick:

**Use Habit Stacking to take advantage of your brain:**

When we say that our minds are "lazy," what we're saying is that they like to maintain the status quo. Thanks to a process that occurs as we age called synaptic pruning, our brains build more reliable connections between neurons each time we repeat the behavior. The more you do something, the easier it becomes (with less energy). While this is great for your good habits, it means your brain removes or "prunes" connections to patterns you don't use. When it comes to building practices, you must "use them or lose them." A significant advantage of established connections is that they're excellent starting points for new habits. Researchers have discovered that we can take advantage of our current patterns to build new ones.

**Building confidence:**

Focus on your strengths. Nothing strips people of more confidence than trying to improve their weaknesses. Improving weaknesses is one of the biggest lies in the world. Wherever you're weak, surround yourself people who have that strength. To become unbreakable, think about your past successes. Remember the last time you felt unstoppable. What made you feel invincible? You felt that way because you were charging on all cylinders; you were harnessing your strengths. You've never felt unstoppable while working on your weaknesses. Working on weaknesses is frustrating, and it's programmed into you by traditional education when you take a variety of useless classes. Many schools try to fit students into a one-size-fits-all model. It doesn't work. You don't need well-rounded education; you only need to focus on and hone your natural strengths. Do you know what happens when you master your exceptional qualities? People who are weak at it pay you—a lot. Would you like to become ok at a *long-list* of things, or wealthy from a *short-list* of things? What are you so good at, it's as natural as breathing? Those are your strengths. Remember, whatever it is, it's not easy for plenty of people, and they'll trade their dollars to you for it. Live in your strengths and be unbreakable.

**Start incredibly small:**

To maintain habits, give them the best foundation and begin with mico-steps. *Think* big, *start* small. Many people get impatient and try to start at the end. These are the people who go from never working out to doing six days a week or the investors who want to buy an apartment complex when they've never purchased a house. Think of your life as a boat and captain a speedboat before you captain the cruise ship. When you start as the speedboat, you have the agility to maneuver away from danger. If you're heading towards the rocks, you can turn away. Now, imagine you're the cruise ship. If you're heading towards rocks, all you can do is brace for impact. The "cruise ships" are those that make $150,000 and spend $160,000. Every time they make more, they spend more; their lives are one missed pay period from bankruptcy.

The speed boats are building up to the "cruise ship," they didn't start there. Because they chose to begin small, they learn to control and add on to their boat. Day after day, month after month, they master the controls and become a yacht. Wealth and success work the same way because you're using your *time* to progress, learning to control more substantial wealth and prosperity. Warren Buffett built his fortune from the ground-up and learned to control billions. Lottery winners start with the "cruise ship" and lose it because they never learned to control the speed boat. Start incredibly small and take care of a cat before you take care of a lion.

**Isolate triggers and rewards by testing them out:**

Rewards are where the change of habit forms. Researchers test a hypothesis until there's evidence supporting the cause. If you think you're drinking Red Bulls because you're tired, then perform a test. Are you more tired in the morning? If you're not tired, do you still crave a Red Bull? You have to reflect on yourself and evaluate each behavior. Test each hypothesis for about a week before you can officially remove it. If you start going to bed earlier, feel less tired, and don't crave a Red Bull, then you understand the trigger and the reward. But, "old habits die hard" is still an accurate phrase. Just because you feel less dependent on Red Bull and you've found the right trigger, doesn't mean a change is automatic. You still have to work to change your behavior based on your thoughts.

**Celebrate your little victories:**

Most people punish themselves for poor performance, and avoid spoiling themselves for achievements. Don't take the *stick* over the *carrot*. Research has shown that celebrating your progress is crucial to your motivation. When you progress, allow yourself to feel it. Stop, pamper yourself, and appreciate how you've grown from your victory. Let's begin this habit immediately, what can you stop and celebrate right now if you had to choose one thing? *Choose something* and then *give something* to yourself. Anything you select will work because you're practicing reinforcing your behavior. You deserve to feel elite because you are.

**Remind yourself:**

Enter reminders to implement your new habit every day; you mustn't miss days. If you waste time by getting sidetracked, the purpose of starting a new practice is frustrated. Use your calendar and your phone timer to help keep you accountable to yourself. Remember earlier, when we set a daily gratitude reminder? When you pick your new habit, choose the most flexible time to practice it every day. What time are you least likely to blow off practice? You can practice by waking up 1 hour earlier than usual or going to bed 1 hour later. That's seven extra hours per week, 365 extra hours per year, devoted to yourself. With your reminder, create a note that reminds you *why* you're practicing every day. Use the seven-levels deep exercise from earlier, along with your calendar, to propel you to the results you want.

**Increase momentum:**

Momentum's your best friend. As you build momentum, you'll gain more energy, which reflects in your self-confidence. Start incredibly small, and you'll develop it from little victories. As you reach your habit development goals daily, they lay the foundation for the significant cause you're building. The "too-small-to-fail" habit comes into play because starting little builds your momentum. You'll move through your days without feeling like compromising. You won't give up because your pattern is so simple that almost no effort's required. You're sculpting the neural pathways in your mind, which help shape your habits. Every habit you have now (good or bad) started small and gave you momentum in a specific direction. The biggest problem is that we try to *spring* before *crawling*. Things don't happen overnight, but we wish they would. Though we live in a society of instant gratification, everything won't happen instantly. Still, everything that takes time is more valuable. What's the smallest action you can take right now towards a habit you want? Go right now, and get your first victory!

# Importance of having successful habits

Human beings are, by nature, creatures of habit. 45% of our reported activities every day are patterns, and they carry on automatically. These unconscious habits are an essential foundation for productivity. The emergence of superhuman levels of self-discipline is simply a collection of healthy habits, carefully cultivated over time. Overnight success is a myth marketed by biographies that spare you the boring details of the time spent in the "gym." Half of our daily actions depend on the situation; we perform them unconsciously. Our perception of control is an illusion, designed to protect our ego and transform a messy reality into a cleaner narrative. Habits are what allow us to function in the world. If we were aware of the millions of micro-decisions we make every day, we'd never get anywhere. Imagine having to assess the pros and cons of behaviors like breathing or walking. Any decision made comes at an opportunity cost for all of our other choices. The fewer decisions we make per day, the more cognitive resources we have. Focus your cognitive resources on only the most crucial decisions. Habits allow our brains to outsource some of the hard decision-making in our environment. As practices become more automatic, neural activity moves from the prefrontal cortex to the basal ganglia. The basal ganglia, which is one of the oldest structures in our brain, is exempt from the thought process.

Habits are beneficial, and it would be impossible to live without them. They automate many of our routines and free our minds to focus on high-level activities. For example, if we thought consciously about essential functions like walking, chewing, or talking, we would have no mental capacity available to perform other tasks. The ability to write, or write automatically, allows us to focus on producing a great article, letter, email, or novel. Similarly, having automatic processes enables us to think about where we're going. We have thousands of these "habits" that our muscle memory has accumulated over time; breathing, for instance. However, driving a car and riding a bike is a series of actions that we also do without conscious intention. So, habits play an essential role in simplifying our lives by reducing the bandwidth we need to use.

Habits are at the center of your success and failures. Humans are habitual creatures, and our brains love to automate sequences to create routines; we want to save space for essential decision-making. When we feel good, we release a chemical called dopamine. However, when we feel bad, it's a steroid hormone called cortisol. Routines have a positive or negative effect on our health and well-being, depending on what our brains are releasing (dopamine or cortisol).

For this reason, it's vital to form habits that improve our lives rather than those with adverse effects. Your ability to collect and master positive habits will shape your results automatically. Practice the habits you've learned, start small, focus on one (no more than two) daily habits consistently. You'll get the results you want (on autopilot). You no longer need to follow step by step processes that don't work; there's no memorization and no more frustration. You're here for a reason, you're a blessing to humanity, and you must use your gifts to enrich the lives of others.

# Conclusion

Everyone wants to be successful. Whether it's getting good grades, getting a promotion, or selling your first novel, we crave it. However, progress is different for everyone. Your success in life is determined, in part, by the choices you make daily, also known as your habits. Habits are powerful; they define who we are and control the direction of our life.

We're creatures of habit. Everything we think, do, and say is the result of patterns deeply rooted in our minds through years of repetitive behavior. Those same habits help us move forward or stop our progress in life. The quality and state of our life right now is a direct reflection of our daily habits. Habits are an undeniably significant part of life. They are an integral part of our behavioral psychology. Use this knowledge to take stock of your patterns, and set yourself in motion to get the results you want.

You deserve freedom; you deserve success, you deserve fulfillment, and the world deserves to experience you at your pinnacle. Nothing in your life is set in stone unless you *decide* it is, and nobody can control your thoughts. Think success, feel like a success, act like a success, and take your victories.

On the next page is a sample of the first chapter of my book, "You Are Rich." I've included it because I want to overdeliver and see you achieve breakthroughs in your life.

I'm proud of you, and I look forward to reading your review!

With gratitude,

Wes Lee

# BONUS: You Are Rich

# CHAPTER ONE: MIND CONTROL

*"You can only control two things in your life: Your attitude and your actions."  Darren Hardy*

Our ability to feel stems from our minds. The mind's often referred to as the seat of consciousness and thought, the very place of our cognitive awareness and imagination. The power and importance of the brain are absolute. Your mind controls your physical expressions, manifestations, and actions. Logical deduction says that the ability to control our mind will cause a radical change in the wellness and effectiveness of anyone.

Here's a classic example of the mind's potent influence on our success and well-being. Have you ever heard of the PLACEBO effect? A placebo effect is a fake treatment believed to be real. Doctors track patients for changes in behavior such as elevated moods and more energy. The doctor assures the patient that they'll improve. The patients' mind subconsciously believes a lie, which becomes their reality. When patients start to feel better, they get pumped up and excited about this improvement. The improvement tricks them into believing the fake drug works. Their strengthened belief, more often than not, increases the effect of the treatment until they feel cured.

Your *intention* is a robust tool that can take on a life of its own to effect radical change. Understanding that the subconscious mind controls the expression of the physical is crucial to determining your success. Thinking with *intention* is not just hypothetical. It is more than just a seat of consciousness; it is the power that drives action, will, and grit.

The subconscious mind is the sum of what we see, hear, say, and believe. Think of it like food. Some people feed their minds with "candy," others fill themselves with "apples." These people aren't totally to blame, because it comes from their childhood. Imagine a child that grew up in a family who eats two meals a day. It's typical for that child to be subconsciously satisfied with two meals a day. They *see* it as being normal; why would they change? What we see and experience <u>shackles</u> or <u>elevates</u> us.

While we're the expression of what we see, you should know that the mind's also influenced by what you say and hear. Ultimately, we're the ones that control our mind; we control what enters the brain and how it functions. We are the god of our thought process, our consciousness, and our imagination.

# Next Steps

# Also by Wes Lee

Impactful Leadership

You Have A Purpose

You Are Rich

You Are Free

Professional Persuasion

The Brave Bunch (Children's Book)

Read more at amazon.com/author/wes_lee

# About the Author

Wes Lee is a passionate advocate for success with over a decade of experience and a business degree from Hawaii Pacific University. Best known for his Leadership in the Army and operating multiple successful businesses, including lending money in 42 states, starting a business that significantly reduces health-care costs, and taking ownership in a life insurance company. Lee's books take his hard-won experience and translate it into easy recipes you can follow to achieve massive breakthroughs. His site https://twitter.com/wes_lee_success shares strategies and resources to have everything you want from life while getting paid handsomely. Wes loves living in Kapolei, Hawaii (a personal dream) with his wife and digging his toes in the sand at the lagoons of Ko'olina.

Follow at
https://www.tiktok.com/@weslee1988